Cher Ami

Cher Ami

Based on the World War I Legend of the Fearless Pigeon

Written by
Mélisande Potter

Illustrated by
Giselle Potter

Christy Ottaviano Books
Little, Brown and Company
New York Boston

A little pigeon named Cher Ami lived on a farm in England.

Every day she flew up into the clear blue sky with her friends. Round and round they soared in a wide circle, before diving home again in single file.

Cher Ami adventured far above
meadows and streams, over rooftops
and the tallest trees, but she always
knew how to return home. She
was a true homing pigeon!

Those peaceful days came to an abrupt halt when the First World War began and Cher Ami was called to duty.

Pigeons were known to be fast fliers, able to deliver messages like mail carriers of the sky. Now Cher Ami and hundreds of other pigeons were needed as messengers to help the United States Army.

At a training camp in France, Cher Ami marched in line, left-right-left-right.

Her trainer put a folded note into a tiny metal
canister and fastened it to her leg.

Then he scooped her into his big hands and tossed her in the direction of her new coop across a field.

The lesson to deliver a message worked well, and
Cher Ami's dinner was waiting there for her.

Cher Ami showed great skill, practicing several hours each day to fly farther and faster.

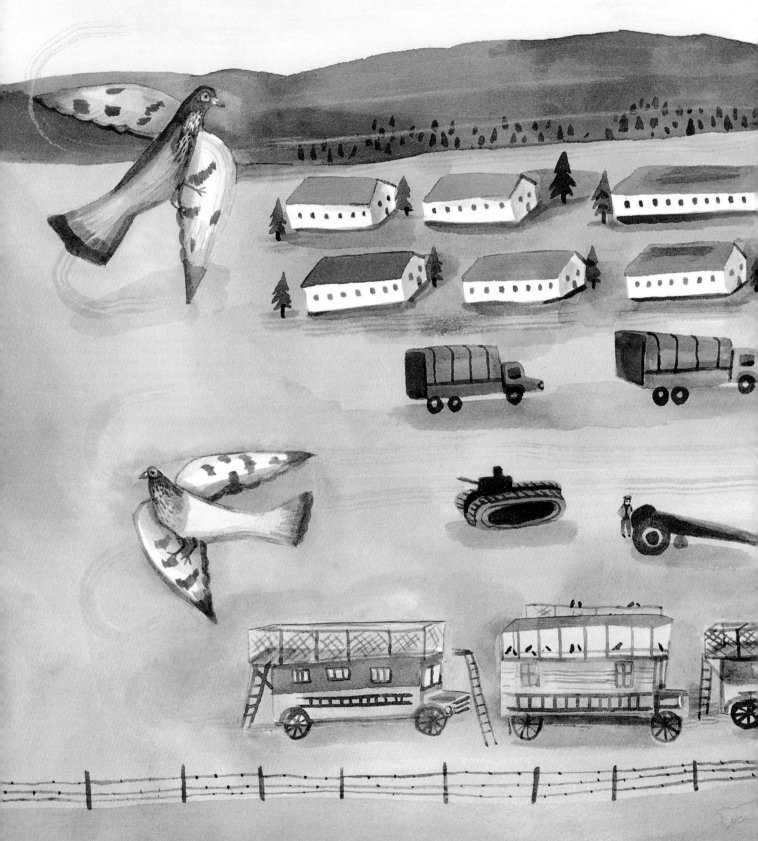

In just a few days, she could travel long distances
at nearly fifty miles an hour!

On a crisp, cold morning in October, Cher Ami was among six hundred messenger pigeons sent to the war's front lines. American troops were already there to help French soldiers win the war.

When the birds arrived, everything felt strange.

The sky was dark, with frightening sounds and bullets spraying all around. Each boom and bang was deafening. Cher Ami was not afraid. She was given her first order to deliver a message—and she was ready!

Off she flew in the middle of bursting bombs and blinding flashes of light. Cher Ami struggled to fly above the range of fire, determined to succeed. Her eyes hurt from the clouds of smoke, and it was difficult to breathe. With great courage, she raced at top speed until she reached her home loft.

The soldiers greeted her with cheers—and her dinner too.
A day-old baguette had never tasted so good!

Cher Ami was tired but unstoppable. She completed twelve dangerous missions, carrying secret messages between troops and their commanders. It was a huge and risky task to keep army information away from enemy hands.

The worst day came when American soldiers were trapped in a ravine surrounded by enemy gunfire. Their own troops did not know their location and were mistakenly firing at them along with the enemy. They were desperate to contact their headquarters for help before more lives were lost. After two other pigeons failed to deliver the soldiers' message, Cher Ami was their only hope.

She flew fast with the urgent message, only this time the enemy spotted her. Shots echoed over land like a thunderstorm as bullets whizzed past Cher Ami, one after another.

Pow!

A stinging pain in her chest made her tumble toward the ground. She was badly wounded. Soldiers watched in horror as she stopped moving. They shouted pleas for her to continue her mission.

Then, suddenly, Cher Ami struggled to take flight.
She would not give up! Her whole body ached as she tried
to lift her wings. It seemed incredible when she flapped
them fast enough to rise again, higher than ever!

With all her might, she pushed forward
through the sky for twenty-five miles, alone
like a little boat in a big, dark sea.

Exhausted, Cher Ami had arrived at the home loft. She lay as still as a stone. It was a sad sight for the soldier who found her. Poor Cher Ami was covered in blood and had a hole in her chest.

There, dangling from what was left of her leg, hung the message that would help save 194 soldiers on the battlefield.

PIGEON MESSAGE

WE ARE ALONG THE ROAD
PARALELL 276.4. OUR ARTILLERY
IS DROPPING A BARRAGE
DIRECTLY ON US.

FOR HEAVENS SAKE
STOP IT.

*Rendering of authentic message

Now it was time to save Cher Ami. For many hours, an army
veterinarian tended to her wounds. They were able to save her life
but not her leg. A grateful soldier carved her a new one from a tree
twig, which fit over her tiny stump.

This courageous pigeon had well earned her name *Cher Ami*, which means "dear friend" in French. She was instantly declared a hero and soon became known all over the world.

When she was well enough to travel, Cher Ami returned to America. She had flown like a fierce wind to rescue many soldiers and would now become an honored mascot of the United States Army.

As the boat began to pull away, she stood proudly in the spotlight of the sun. She was the most unforgettable, fearless little pigeon, Cher Ami.

A Note from the Author

This telling of Cher Ami's story is a blend of truth and legend. Some facts remain unclear, but what is certain is that Cher Ami was a courageous pigeon.

World War I, called the Great War, was fought from 1914 to 1918. The outbreak was caused by the assassination of Franz Ferdinand, archduke of Austria-Hungary, over his power and land wealth. Europe split into two groups: the Allies (France, Great Britain, Italy, Russia, and later the United States) and the Central Powers (Germany, Austria-Hungary, Bulgaria, and Turkey). With the added strength of the United States Army in 1917, the Allies won the war.

During World War I, homing pigeons were invaluable. They could fly as fast as fifty miles per hour, making them a quick method of communication. Radios were not as dependable.

In October 1918, a "Lost Battalion" of 694 American soldiers was isolated by German troops in the Argonne Forest of France. Cher Ami's mission helped save 194 men. The soldiers were part of the 77th Division, which was mostly made up of New York City's immigrant community. African American soldiers also fought in the war, in segregated units.

Cher Ami was born in April 1918 and died on June 13, 1919, the date that would become celebrated as International Pigeon Appreciation Day. Although pigeons can live up to fifteen years, their life span varies depending on their daily routines. Cher Ami's life was short, but her list of achievements is long.

Cher Ami was assumed to be a male pigeon. After she died, the taxidermist was preparing her to be mounted when he discovered that Cher Ami was, in fact, female! She is displayed at the Smithsonian's National Museum of American History to be remembered forever.

Cher Ami was awarded the Croix de Guerre medal, inducted into the Racing Pigeon Hall of Fame, won a gold medal from the Organized Bodies of American Pigeon Fanciers for her extraordinary and heroic service during World War I, and in 2019 received the Animals in War & Peace Medal of Bravery.

A Note from the Artist

I spent a lot of time researching Cher Ami, poring over photographs taken during World War I of soldiers and homing pigeons, yet my pictures of Cher Ami's story are not always depicted with full accuracy. To highlight a tiny pigeon in the giant setting of World War I, I needed to make some adjustments. For instance, pigeons were often loaded onto ships in crates rather than in wire cages and carried in baskets that were not as transparent as I painted them, but I felt it was important for Cher Ami to remain focal. Of course, real pigeons don't march in line like soldiers, but in a picture book they can! It is not certain that Cher Ami wore the wooden leg that a soldier had carved for her, but I loved imagining that she did. A small pigeon would not be noticeable on a huge ship or sit on a railing uncaged, and crowds of fans probably didn't gather to wave goodbye as her boat pulled away, but I wanted Cher Ami to be visible, larger than life, and recognized as the true hero that she was.

Sources

Alamy Stock Photo. "'British Army Carrier Pigeons in France' (1919). Creator: Unknown." www.alamy.com/british-army-carrier-pigeons-in-france-1919-creator-unknown-image246382359.html.

Animals in War and Peace. "MOB #2—Cher Ami (WW1)." waranimals.com/2019-mob-recipients.

Bieniek, Adam. "Cher Ami: The Pigeon That Saved the Lost Battalion." World War One Centennial Commission. www.worldwar1centennial.org/index.php/communicate/press-media/wwi-centennial-news/1210-cher-ami-the-pigeon-that-saved-the-lost-battalion.html.

Laplander, Robert J. *Finding the Lost Battalion*. Self-published, Lulu Press, 2006.

Laplander, Robert J. "Lost Battalion." World War One Centennial Commission. www.worldwar1centennial.org/index.php/233-lost-battalion.html.

National Archives Catalog. "Signal Corps Activities, Homing Pigeons [France, 1918]." 1936. catalog.archives.gov/id/25003.

Parting Words. "Cher Ami: The Brave Pigeon That Saved 200 Lives." parting-words.com/story/cher-ami.

Science Source. "WWI, U.S. Army Signal Corps Carrier Pigeon." www.sciencesource.com/CS.aspx?VP3=SearchResult&ITEMID=SS2603835.

Serena, Katie. "Cher Ami Saved 200 Men During World War I—She Was Also a Pigeon." All That's Interesting. January 30, 2019. allthatsinteresting.com/cher-ami.

Smithsonian Institution. "Cher Ami." www.si.edu/object/cher-ami:nmah_425415.

Staveley-Wadham, Rose. "'The Feathered Battalions'—The Brave Pigeons of Wartime." The British Newspaper Archive. July 3, 2020. blog.britishnewspaperarchive.co.uk/2020/07/03/brave-pigeons-of-wartime.

World War One Centennial Commission. "Lost Battalion—Myths and Legends." www.worldwar1centennial.org/index.php/234-lost-battalion/lost-battalion-myths-and-legends.html.

For Pia, Izzy, Adelita, and Felix —MP

For Mom —GP

About This Book

The illustrations for this book were done in watercolor and ink on paper. This book was edited by Christy Ottaviano and designed by Karina Granda. The production was supervised by Ruiko Tokunaga, and the production editor was Jen Graham. The text was set in Century Schoolbook, and the display type is hand drawn.

Text copyright © 2022 by Mélisande Potter • Illustrations copyright © 2022 by Giselle Potter • Cover illustration copyright © 2022 by Giselle Potter • Cover design by Karina Granda • Cover copyright © 2022 by Hachette Book Group, Inc. • Hachette Book Group supports the right to free expression and the value of copyright. The purpose of copyright is to encourage writers and artists to produce the creative works that enrich our culture. • The scanning, uploading, and distribution of this book without permission is a theft of the author's intellectual property. If you would like permission to use material from the book (other than for review purposes), please contact permissions@ hbgusa.com. Thank you for your support of the author's rights. • Little, Brown and Company • Hachette Book Group • 1290 Avenue of the Americas, New York, NY 10104 • Visit us at LBYR.com • First Edition: May 2022 • Christy Ottaviano Books is an imprint of Little, Brown and Company. • The Christy Ottaviano Books name and logo are trademarks of Hachette Book Group, Inc. • The publisher is not responsible for websites (or their content) that are not owned by the publisher. • Library of Congress Cataloging-in-Publication Data • Names: Potter, Mélisande, author. | Potter, Giselle, illustrator. • Title: Cher Ami : based on the World War I legend of the fearless pigeon / by Mélisande Potter ; illustrated by Giselle Potter. • Description: First edition. | New York : Christy Ottaviano Books ; Little, Brown and Company, 2022. | Audience: Ages 4–8 | Summary: "A nonfiction picture book about the unforgettable Cher Ami, a heroic animal who changed WWI history forever." —Provided by publisher. • Identifiers: LCCN 2021012371 | ISBN 9780316335348 (hardcover) • Subjects: LCSH: Cher Ami (Pigeon)—Juvenile literature. | World War, 1914–1918—Communications—Juvenile literature. | Homing pigeons—War use—United States— History—20th century—Juvenile literature. • Classification: LCC D639.P45 P68 2022 | DDC 940.4/12730929— dc23 • LC record available at https://lccn.loc.gov/2021012371 • ISBN 978-0-316-33534-8 • PRINTED IN CHINA • APS • 10 9 8 7 6 5 4 3 2 1